This Book
Belongs To:

_____

_____

WE WISH YOU Merry Christmas & HAPPY NEW YEAR

Day #1

I wear a suit of red, with a beard snowy white,

I bring joy to the world on a magical night,

With reindeer and presents, I travel the skies,

Bringing laughter and cheer, as I soar high and fly.

Day #2

I have antlers so grand, and a nose that does glow,

Guiding Santa's sleigh through the night's wintry snow,

With hooves that go patter on rooftops above,

Who am I, spreading kindness and love?

Day #3

Tall and adorned, with baubles that gleam,

I stand in your home like a festive dream,

With lights that twinkle and ornaments bright,

What am I, bringing holiday delight?

Day #4

I fall from the sky, unique and divine,

In intricate patterns, I gracefully twine,

I blanket the earth in a soft, icy sheen,

What am I, in winter's magical scene?

Day #5

I'm Santa's little helper, both mischievous and sly,

In your home, I spy with my watchful eye,

Each night I roam, a new spot I find,

What am I, bringing a sense of Christmas kind?

Day #6

I'm made of sweet dough, with icing so neat,

Children decorate me, a tasty retreat,

With gumdrops and candies, on roofs I'm adorned,

What am I, a treat that's joyfully adorned?

Day #7

I'm striped and curved, with peppermint taste,

A holiday treat, no one can waste,

Hang me on trees, or savor my delight,

What am I, bringing sweetness to the night?

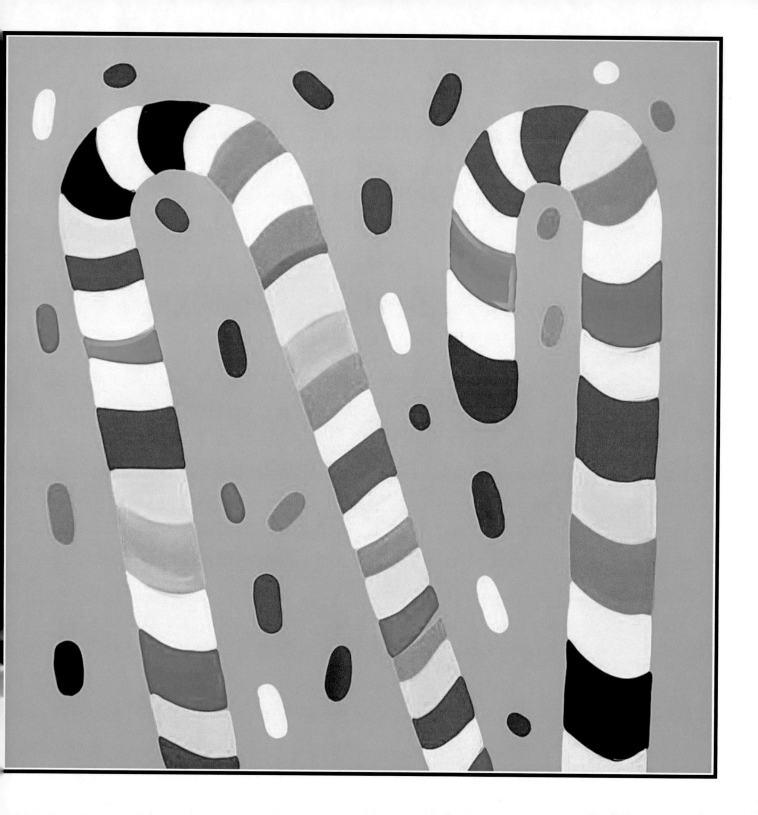

Day #8

I'm hung by the fireplace, a festive delight,

Filled with small treasures on Christmas night,

Children eagerly peek, with eyes all aglow,

What am I, in a home's holiday show?

Day #9

On snowy trails, I glide and I slide,

With jingling bells, on a thrilling ride,

Drawn by horses or reindeer so grand,

What am I, in winter's wonderland?

Day #10

I'm warm and creamy, with marshmallows on top,

On chilly nights, I make hearts stop,

A cozy drink, to sip by the fire,

What am I, that many desire?

Day #11

I twinkle and shimmer, in colors so bright,

In the dark winter, I bring endless light,

Wrapped 'round the tree or hung high and low,

What am I, with a festive glow?

Day #12

I'm crafted from snow, with a carrot for a nose,

Children dress me in scarves and cozy clothes,

With coal for eyes and a hat on my head,

What am I, a friend in snow so widespread?

Day #13

I'm sung by the choir, in harmonious cheer,

During the season, everyone can hear,

With melodies sweet and lyrics so bright,

What am I, bringing joy through the night?

Day #14

I'm paper and ribbons, and a tape's gentle fold,

Hiding surprises, a sight to behold,

Tied up with care, beneath the tree's sprawl,

What am I, concealing gifts big and small?

Day #15

I play on the screen, with stories so merry,

Filled with laughter, or sometimes a fairy,

Characters dance through scenes so grand,

What am I, in your holiday land?

Day #16

I'm sweet and I'm baked, in shapes so divine,

With icing and sprinkles, on each design,

From gingerbread men to stars up above,

What am I, a treat that everyone loves?

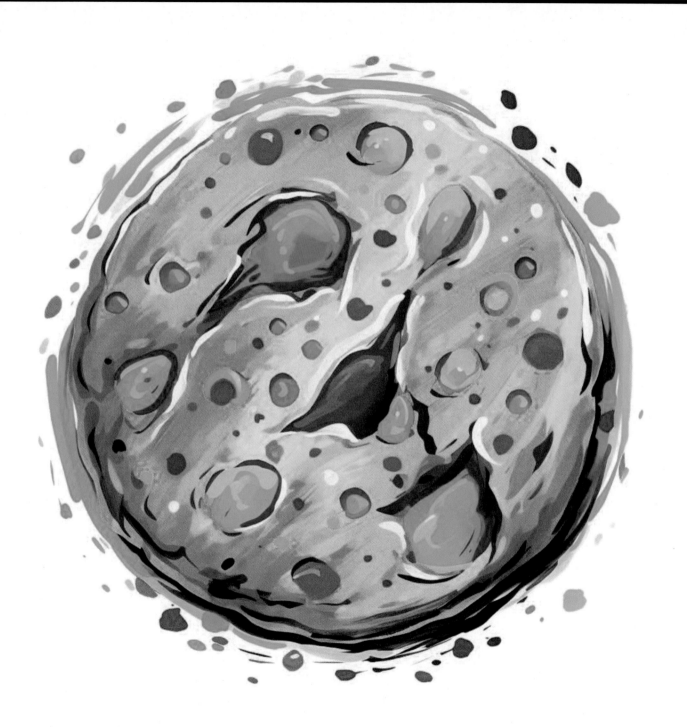

Day #17

I'm hung from the ceiling, a plant above,

A symbol of love, and holiday love,

Underneath me, people find bliss,

What am I, in a moment of kiss?

Day #18

I glide on the ice, with elegance and grace,

In the winter wonderland, I find my place,

With blades on my feet, I twirl and I spin,

What am I, in a world frozen thin?

Day #19

I count down the days, with doors to unveil,

Each morning a surprise, in a small hidden trail,

From chocolates to toys, behind each small gate,

What am I, in the holiday date?

Day #20

I'm paper and glue, with scissors that snip,

Children create me, with a joyful grip,

From ornaments to cards, in colors so bright,

What am I, a creation of delight?

Day #21

I bring friends together, with laughter and cheer,

In festive attire, we gather near,

With games and treats, and music that plays,

What am I, brightening up winter days?

Day #22

In a land of dreams, with a uniform so grand,

I guard the treasures, with a key in my hand,

In a magical ballet, I come to life in advance,

What am I, with a nutcracking stance?

Day #23

In gardens lush, where flowers bloom,

I'm a tiny creature with plenty of room,

With a pointy hat and a merry smile,

What am I, in the garden aisle?

Day #24

Inside a glass sphere, a magical sight,

A snowy scene, so pure and white,

When shaken, it snows, a miniature dance,

What am I, in a winter's enchanting trance?

All The answers are here!

SCAN HERE!

Made in the USA
Monee, IL
03 December 2023